Table of Contents

ISBN-13: 978-0-692-18733-3

Introduction

For patients and customers seeking information as cannabis becomes more accessible, it's beneficial to understand how to use cannabis to improve health and well-being.

Information presented in these pages is intended to help build an understanding of how the body functions, develops, and heals. This manual is a collection of experience, insights, and information publicly available.

Thousands of years of empirical evidence has allowed generations of healers to discover the medicinal properties of plants. The love involved in nurturing, harvesting, preparing, and using plants is what connects people to each other and the earth. Modern science has been rediscovering the health benefits of cannabis.

Cannabis is one of many tools for well-being and can be integrated into a healthy lifestyle through conscious consumption and responsible use. Balanced diet, enjoyable exercise, and relaxation enhance the medicinal benefits, effects, and absorption of plant medicine.

Plants and herbs can be used as part of disease prevention, intervention, or recovery with the ultimate goal of transitioning to positive thinking, relaxation, self-empowerment, and healthy happy habits. If a person loses the ability to produce bliss hormones, then using plant medicine can stimulate production of joyful chemicals that eliminate stress and help restore balance.

Nervous System

It is impossible to separate the organs in our body into mutually exclusive functions. The mind, body, emotions, and organs have an influence and impact on each other. The brain is the communication center of the body and part of a vast, interconnected system, with a team of organs communicating through an omnipresent network of nerves.

The nervous system connects the brain to every organ function. Nerves in the brain give rise to cognitive function and allow us to think and control movement. Nerves in our body facilitate involuntary responses and are part of unconscious processes such as breathing, digestion, and heartbeat. Nerves in our skin and sensory organs relay messages from the environment. The body is influenced physically by our environment as chemicals and electrical signals release in response to touch, smell, light, noise, and taste.

Psychoneuroimmunology studies the interaction between psychological processes and the nervous and immune system. The mind, body, emotions, and environment are interlinked. Being happy boosts the immune system. Being relaxed regulates the nervous system and promotes healing. Being depressed or anxious weakens the immune system and increases the likelihood of disease.

The nervous system conserves energy and promotes healing when the relaxation response is active. High amounts of stress mobilize the body, divert regular organ function, and interrupt the ability to think, learn, and heal.

Significant Relations

Central nervous system connects the brain and spinal cord.

> **Cranial** nerves travel from the brain to the eyes, mouth, ears, and other parts of the head.
>
> **Spinal** nerves travel from the spinal cord to other parts of the body.

Glial cells surround neurons to support and protect nerves.

Peripheral nervous system connects our central nervous system to our limbs and organs.

> **Autonomic** nervous system connects our spinal cord to our lungs, heart, gut, bladder, and reproductive organs controlling involuntary actions.
>
>> **Parasympathetic** nerves conserve energy and promote healing during rest.
>>
>> **Sympathetic** nerves mobilize the body during flight-fight-or-freeze response.
>
> **Somatic** nerves control our voluntary muscle movement.
>
> **Enteric** nerves control functions in the gastrointestinal system.

Neurotransmitter Systems

Individual nerve cells, or neurons, are specialized to send and receive signals rapidly. They use electrical impulses and chemicals to communicate between the brain, body, and organs. Neurons form pathways that affect development, learning ability, and decision-making.

Neurotransmitters are chemical messengers in our nervous system that stimulate the flight-fight-freeze response, enable relaxation and recovery, and sustain vital organ functions. They manifest internally and are accessed through a balanced diet.

Transmitters control receptors to stimulate the production of enzymes, pain channel blockers, and hormones that control the response and reaction of cells and organs. They affect us physically and psychologically as the source of all emotion. Transmitters enact changes in gene expression to activate cell response. Over time, it leads to epigenetic changes that are inherited by offspring.

Epigenetics researches how genes change in response to our environment, habitual patterns, and hereditary factors. DNA and biological chemistry changes in response to the environment over time.

The transmission of chemicals throughout the body is complex. Synergy between substances is still being established. Sometimes 1+1=2. Other times 1+1=0, or even 10. Neurotransmitters can work together or in opposition with other transmitters.

Significant Relations

Precursors to neurotransmitters require vitamins from our diet or sunlight to develop.

Agonist Receptors work to activate chemical transmission and initiate reaction. Direct agonists, such as THC, nicotine, and opioids activate receptors and bind directly to target sites. Indirect agonists increase the number of neurotransmitters through preventing reuptake. Agonists can work together to enhance effects or compete for receptors if used together.

Antagonist Receptors act to reduce the activity of another chemical. Direct antagonists work to fit in and block the space intended for transmitters. Indirect antagonists impede the production of neurotransmitters. Agonists and antagonists can work synergistically or in opposition. CBD works to balance the effects of THC.

Acetylcholine System controls motor nerves to activate muscles. It also plays a role in neuromodulation to activate slow-acting receptors and is important in alertness, arousal, motivation, attention, and memory. It helps us wake up in the morning and sustain attention for memory and learning. High levels are associated with convulsions and restlessness, while low levels contribute to dementia, weakness and fatigue. Nicotine, THC, and muscimol mushrooms bind to receptors in this system. Stretching, meditation, and moderate exercise help balance receptor activity.

Adenosine System supports sleep and suppresses arousal or wakefulness. It regulates bone and blood flow and hair growth. Caffeine blocks adenosine receptors, which increases dopamine and glutamate activity.

Adrenaline System stimulates our body during fight-or-flight in times of fear. It increases blood flow to muscles, pupil dilation, and blood sugar. Adrenaline enhances long-term memory formation leading to post-traumatic stress and flashbacks. Adrenaline is a major detriment to homeostasis.

Dopamine System influences our reward-motived behavior. It provides alertness, cognitive control, pain sensation and working memory alongside noradrenaline. Dopamine motivates us towards our goals and acts as a positive reinforcement when successful. Breaking down goals and creating new ones before achieving current ones ensures a constant sense of accomplishment. Dopamine increases blood flow and regulates activity in the gastrointestinal and immune system. CBD, opium, cocaine and endorphins affect dopamine receptors. Low levels of dopamine are associated with procrastination and self-doubt.

Endocannabinoid System regulates physiological and cognitive processing including fertility, mood, appetite, pain sensation, memory, development of neurons, bone regeneration, and learning ability. It restores a state of balance, or homeostasis, in the immune system, reduces pain, and is responsible for exercise and meditation-induced euphoria. Endocannabinoid receptors are wide-spread and impact many other neurotransmitter systems. Anandamide is the main endocannabinoid commonly referred to as the "bliss" hormone, which inhibits norepinephrine. THC activates receptors in the endocannabinoid system to provide euphoria and relaxation. CBD works as indirectly on cannabinoid receptors.

Glutamate System is responsible for neural communication, memory formation, neural regulation, and learning. It is the main excitatory neurotransmitter in the brain and overstimulation can cause neurodegeneration or mental disorders. Glutamate receptors are mainly found on neurons and glial cells. Glial cells help maintain homeostasis and provide support and protection to neurons. They are the "glue" to the nervous system. Glutamate is ordinally obtained through our diet. Ketamine effects our glutamate receptors. Dysfunction is associated with numerous neurological disorders including aching, autism, diabetes, MS, Parkinson's, schizophrenia, and seizures.

Glucocorticoid System controls steroids, cortisol, and regulates inflammation. Cortisol is released in times of stress or low blood sugar to suppress the immune system and decrease bone formation. At normal levels, cortisol is essential to sustaining life and supports our heart, immune system, fetal development, homeostasis, and metabolism. Cognitively, it affects our vivid memory and vigilance.

Histamine System is involved in inflammation, local immune response, and gut regulation. It also mediates the itching reflex, allergic reactions, and provides homeostasis in the endocrine system. Histamine promotes alertness, blood flow, coughing, sneezing, low blood pressure, and white blood cell function. Like other neurotransmitters, it is involved in memory and learning.

Meridian System is part of Traditional Chinese Medicine and are pathways through which energy flows. Each organ system has a pathway to communicate with other organs and related structures. Acupuncturists follow points along the meridian.

Norepinephrine System mobilizes the brain and body for action. It is lowest during sleep, rises when we wake, and is highest during the stress-triggered flight-or-fight response. It increases our alertness, arousal, memory formation and retrieval, cognitive control, respiration, blood flow, energy, negative emotional memory, and perception of pain. It can also increase anxiety and restlessness and decrease mobility of the gastrointestinal system and bladder. Norepinephrine controls heart rate both during stress and rest.

Opioid System mitigates pain and stress perception. Opioids and endorphin are released in response to acute pain or stress, during exercise, and when laughing. Opioids create a sense of euphoria and satisfaction and are involved in emotions, interpersonal relationships, and hunger. CBD affects opioid receptors to decrease pain and lessen addictive tendencies.

Oxytocin System influences prosocial and sexual bonding behavior. It creates trust from intimacy and helps strengthen relationships. Mothers release oxytocin to induce contractions and from nipple stimulation during breastfeeding. It is commonly referred to as the "love" or "cuddle" hormone released during affectionate touch, long hugs, and orgasm to regulate stress, social memory, recognition, libido, bonding and maternal behavior. Receptors are found in the brain, heart, retina, testicles, cervix, and kidneys. Estrogen increases the release of oxytocin. Testosterone inhibits the release to reduce empathy and increase aggressive behavior. Giving and receiving gifts increases oxytocin levels.

Serotonin System releases chemicals in the brain and gut. It is commonly thought of as a major contributor to happiness and is triggered when we feel significant or important. Serotonin increases gastrointestinal motility and regulates blood clotting, mood, appetite, and sleep. It plays a role in memory, learning, sensory perception, body temperature regulation and wound healing. Serotonin helps relieve nausea and neuropathy pain. CBD, THCV, 5-HTP, MDMA and psychedelics activate serotonin receptors. Loneliness and depression are associated with low levels of serotonin. Practicing gratitude helps boost serotonin.

Vasopressin System regulates water to maintain hydration and increase blood pressure. It is released in circadian rhythms. Vasopressin is involved on mental levels in facial recognition, bonding, and assertiveness. Alcohol influences the vasopressin system.

Circadian rhythm is a process that keeps biological functions in sync. Rhythms or routines take place in accordance to environmental ques such as light, noise, smell and temperature. Many of our neurotransmitters are released in rhythm creating patterns of wakefulness, alertness, and tiredness.

Endocannabinoid System

The endocannabinoid system (ECS) is the most widespread receptor system in the human body. From initiating uterine attachment during conception through releasing growth hormones in adolescence—it plays the most important role in sustaining health and well-being.

The human body constantly undergoes cellular build-up and breakdown. Toxins, free-radicals, and detrimental proteins released in response to stress speed up inflammation, aging and death. Anti-oxidants, cannabinoids and neurotransmitters all work to restore balance through creating a state for cell repair and renewal. After stress, trauma, or injury occurs, the body naturally seeks balance and our cannabinoid receptors increase.

Cannabinoid receptors regulate many important neurotransmitter pathways in the human body. They function to control the flow of signals that are being sent between neurons and cells with the goal of maintaining balance or homeostasis. It stabilizes our brain, bones, organs and immune system.

When the body detects too much build up or break down of cells, it appears to nudge the body back to normal. Endocannabinoids are made and released by cells on-demand in response to a trigger or trauma. The endocannabinoid system determines how your cells try to right themselves when something goes wrong or imbalance occurs. It regulates mood, appetite, memory, and pain sensation. Endocannabinoids are produced during exercise, meditation, laughter, deep breathing, and singing. Phytocannabinoids activate the same CB receptors and are found in cannabis, black pepper, cacao, Japanese liverwort, echinacea, black truffles, kava, and electric daisy, among others.

When using phytocannabinoids, chemotherapy patients find relief from pain and nausea. Opioid patients find a reduction in the amount of medication necessary to relieve symptoms while decreasing their tolerance, reducing side-effects, and eliminating withdrawal. With over five hundred chemicals that interact with every organ system, it's no wonder cannabis treats various medical conditions.

Homeostasis, or harmony, is reached when bliss chemicals called cannabinoids enter our bloodstream. Active stress causes our body to go into fight-flight-or freeze response and disrupts the natural balance. Cannabinoids allow us to stimulate the relaxation response to heal, recover, restore and learn.

Cannabinoids are proven to help protect our brain, create neurons, enhance left and right brain function, and form new pathways for learning. Neurons are usually fully formed by adulthood. Cannabinoids allow for new experiences to take place. When we try new things, we expand our perspective and physically change brain function.

Pets and Children have endocannabinoid systems that can benefit from cannabis use if under dysfunction.

Significant Relations

Endocannabinoids are produced within our brain, heart, kidneys and organs in response to sensory stimulation or diet.

Anandamide and **2AG** are two common endocannabinoids that activate CB1 receptors.

Phytocannabinoids are produced by cannabis and other plants and herbs.

THC, CBD, and Beta-Caryophyllene are three common plant chemicals that directly or indirectly activate ECS receptors.

CB1 Receptors are mainly in the brain and nervous system. Activation affects mood and cognition. THC increases blood flow and opens the airway, but it does not control heart rate or breath—making it impossible to overdose. CB1 receptors can be found in multiple areas of the brain, central nervous system, thyroid, airway, liver, adrenals, uterus, prostate, testes, eye, stomach, pancreas, heart, bones, and digestive tract. CB1 receptors are activated by anandamide, 2AG, and THC and antagonized by THCV.

CB2 Receptors are in the immune system and peripheral organs. CB2 receptors are found in the eye, stomach, heart, pancreas, bones, digestive tract, and skin. Activation increases anti-inflammatory response, neuroprotection and bone development.

TRPV1 Receptors are found in the sensory nerves, blood, bone marrow, and digestive system. Activation reduces the perception of pain. CBD,

CBG, CBGV, and THCV activate TRPV1 receptors.

TRPA1 Receptors are in the skin, muscles, lungs, stomach, and kidneys. CBD, CBC, and CBN activate TRPA1 receptors and reduce the perception of pain.

GPR18 Receptors are in the spinal cord, bone marrow, small intestine, immune cells, testis, lung, and cerebellum. Activation lowers blood pressure and increases immune system function.

GPR55 Receptors are found in the central nervous system, lungs, liver, gastrointestinal tract, and bladder. It regulates energy intake and output. Activation increases anti-inflammatory response and neuroprotection, lowers blood pressure, and can block pain.

GPR119 Receptors are mainly in the pancreas and gastrointestinal tract. Activation increases appetite, regulates blood sugar, and decreases body weight.

Glycine Receptors are in the spine and regulate the transmission of pain to the brain. CBD and THC interact with glycine receptors.

PPA Receptors bind directly to the DNA sequence. Activation increases neuroprotection and metabolism, as well as reducing addiction and tumors. CBD modulates PPA receptors.

Orexin Receptors regulate sleep and appetite.

Chemokine Receptors attract white blood cells to sites of infection and is involved in tumor metastasis.

Biological Chemistry

Biochemistry studies how our metabolism, diet, and environment create chemical reactions which cause the body to absorb and react to plant medicine differently.

Biological chemistry evolves from hereditary and epigenetic changes throughout life. Epigenetic change occurs as neurotransmitters are released in response to environmental signals such as light, temperature, nutrition, or emotion and initiate changes in gene expression.

We inherit genes that have been switched on or off and can be prone to certain disease and illness. Children with ADHD, diabetes, epilepsy, or cancer are born with hereditary imbalances in their biological chemistry. A person can suffer from minor imbalances with the onset of physical or mental illness developing later in life.

Gut flora breaks down amino acids that regulate organ function. Stomach microbiota aids intestinal immune cells and neuroprotection. There are thousands of microbes that play an important role in immune system function. An imbalanced diet and gut microbiome can lead to autoimmune disease, asthma, irritable bowel syndrome ("IBS"), ulcerative colitis, autism, diabetes, rheumatoid arthritis, cancer, obesity, inflammation, MS, and neurodegenerative disease. The gut and brain are connected and communicate through biochemical signaling via the central nervous system initiating epigenetic change.

Chapter 4: Biochemistry

Biochemical cycles work together to sustain organ function. Conscious consumption and balanced diet are essential for healthy living. The organs within our cells and microbiota in our gut cannot function without oxygen, water, carbohydrates, lipids, protein, balanced pH, vitamins and phytonutrients. An imbalance in diet leads to imbalance in our mind and body.

Metabolism encompasses all the chemical reactions our body needs to survive. While metabolism is commonly associated with the intake of food, it has more to do with energy needed for basic functions like keeping the heart beating. Our metabolism is affected by diet, exercise, stress, and genetic makeup. Exercise is important for muscle tone and bone health, but it uses little of our daily intake of calories.

Our greatest control is over what we choose to eat. Essential fatty acids, antioxidants, and certain foods can increase the bioavailability of cannabinoids. Antioxidants have a network effect and work better together.

There are numerous interactions that effect how plant nutrients are absorbed. We each have a unique biochemical system, making it hard to suggest a standard dose, delivery method, or strain. Our metabolism changes throughout the day. The best approach to using cannabis is to follow general guidelines and experiment responsibly.

Significant Relations

Mitochondria are organs within our cells that produces energy. Mitochondria are also involved in cell signaling, cell growth, and death. Light exposure, cold temperature, intermittent fasting, healthy fat, anti-oxidants, low sugar and refined grain diet, movement and exercise all increase the health and function of our mitochondria. Healthy food, good environment, and exercise increase the amount of energy produced by cells. Stress, unhealthy diet, and toxins increase free radicals which are detrimental to health and well-being.

Glucose or blood sugar levels affect mood, energy, and ability to focus and concentrate. The brain demands about a quarter of our daily metabolism and gets most of its energy from glucose. Refined sugar, however, is harmful if consumed regularly in high quantities. Having too much or too little food creates instability in the body. The pancreas, liver, and adrenal glands help regulate blood sugar. Certain cannabinoids also help regulate glucose levels.

Carbohydrates help our cells produce energy. Malnutrition causes the liver to break down muscle to produce more glucose. Eating too many refined and processed simple carbs at once stresses the liver, pancreas, and adrenal glands causing exhaustion and icreased fat production.

Proteins are made up of 9 different amino acids. They serve as a building block for tissue, neurotransmitters, and energy. A plant-based diet provides complete protein with less saturated fat.

Lipids, or fat, does more than store energy. Lipids work in cell signaling and facilitate absorption of certain vitamins. Fat cells line our skin and work as connective tissue and give our organs protection. White fat stores energy and brown fat produces heat. The brain gets its energy from glucose and medium chain fatty acids (MCTs).

Adaptogens are a class of herbs and mushrooms used for centuries to help the body regulate immune function and adapt to stress. Ginsing, ashwagandha, cordyceps, reishi, and cannabis can be taken synergistically to reduce stress.

Antioxidants work to eliminate free-radicals produced by toxins, stress, and unhealthy diet. Antioxidants have a network effect similar to the entourage effect. Cannabinoids work to reduce oxidative stress and effects can be enhanced if taken with other antioxidants. Hemp seed, blueberries, bay leaf, pecans, cacao, goji berries, cranberries, lion's mane, green tea, and spinach are high in antioxidants.

Stress, Dysfunction, and Recovery

Dysfunction of the endocannabinoid system is linked to every chronic medical condition. The ECS can become imbalanced from hereditary traits, trauma, or repetitive stress. Overstimulation or under stimulation interrupts healthy organ system function and prevents healing.

Repetitive stress is toxic, causing disruption in the ECS and promoting physical and mental disease. Chronic stress repeatedly bombards organ systems with adrenaline and cortisol. Ignoring stress causes the body to send increasing amounts of disease-producing proteins resulting in dysfunction. The result is chronic inflammation, immune disorders, bone decay, DNA coding issues, cell death, gastrointestinal issues, blood sugar regulation problems, and an overall imbalance.

The heart and brain are connected through the autonomic nervous system. Our flight-fight-freeze or relaxation response release biochemicals that interact with cells and create epigenetic change.

Being under-stimulated can cause low performance. Certain amounts of motivational stress allow for better performance. Optimal performance is reached when a person is motivated by stress and remains confident. Excess anxiety and self-doubting lead to an overwhelmed state of distress resulting in low performance.

If the body constantly undergoes stress, it overwhelms the natural ability to heal, and pain and inflammation are imminent. Chronic inflammation in response to stress leads to cell death in bones, joints, organs, and nerves.

Plant chemicals only mimic what the body can naturally produce. Gratitude, laughter, love, and relaxation release endocannabinoids to increase happiness, reduce sensitivity to physical symptoms, and inspire healing.

A healthy diet, restful sleep, breathing techniques, meditation, affectionate touch, and exercise provide the stamina and energy necessary to effectively enact and embrace stress. By making simple, positive steps to stay physically healthy, stress can be motivational rather than disruptive.

Restore balance through self-empowerment, plant medicine, laughter, creativity, forgiveness, gratitude, conscious action, and critical thinking.

Thought shapes reality. Neural pathways develop based on actions and create behavioral patterns that teach the body what to expect, avoid, and crave. It can be easy to forget that we ourselves are the most important member of the healing team, and that it is possible to get better and be well. Do not confuse the term *chronic* with *incurable*.

Stress causes depression that leads to illness which causes more stress that deepens depression and worsens the disease. The proverbial snake begins to eat its own tail in the cycle of emotional and physical suffering. A negative mind-set and constricting emotions reduce our ability to protect and heal. If a person can't organically create bliss chemicals, they can become forced to access them through addictive behavior.

The longer we continue to avoid making the changes necessary to deal with stress, the more systemic it becomes. Instead, meet disease with confidence, persistence, and positive thought. It *is* possible to intervene when trapped in a viscous cycle.

Cannabis is non-dependent and non-addictive physiologically. Addiction can affect a person mentally or physically. It takes place when a person seeks out positive reinforcement from external sources without working to restore balance. Unresolved emotional stress and negative thought patterns can lead to self-satisfying and co-dependent tendencies. It is possible to become addicted to smoking, drinking, work, exercise, reading, victimizing, social media, television, sex, relationships, or religion.

The first part of the recovery process is believing that healing and release from physical pain and psychological trauma are possible. That allows a person to shift their perspective, embrace the wisdom of the natural world, and consider cannabis as a bridge to recovery.

There are several practices that are a part of mind-body wellness that help you reshape neural pathways: plant medicine, deep breathing, meditation, massage, and stretching. Such tools allow you to focus your mind and develop your ability to relax and concentrate. They feed the underdeveloped neurotransmitters in the brain and satisfy cravings through the natural production of bliss chemicals.

Cannabis allows us to access cannabinoids and create neurological pathways. Plant-produced cannabinoids interact with our cellular receptors in the exact same way natural endocannabinoids do. Phytocannabinoids replace the missing neurotransmitters and signal the production of bliss molecules that trigger our relaxation response. Harmony is restored, and our body regains balance, allowing healing to take place when we are at ease.

Cannabaceae

Cannabis flowers are overflowing with scent and flavor. It's related to the rose family which also contains strawberries, peaches, apples, almonds, pears, figs, and is a close relative to hops.

Cannabis is a hyperaccumulator and bioregulator. It absorbs chemicals, heavy metals, radiation and toxins from the air, soil, and water. Plants can become toxic and harmful if grown in an unhealthy environment. Organic farming is necessary to ensure cannabis medicine is safe for consumption.

The Cannabaceae family contains about two hundred different species of plant. Of the eleven genera, only one contains the cannabis genre, of which there are only three species. The existing paradigm in botany classifies plants inadequately. *Cannabis sativa* and *Cannabis indica* were named based on their size and leaf pattern and not DNA. The misconception of generalizing cannabis effects into Sativa, Indica, and Hybrid continues to fade as more consumers and patients learn more about terpenes. The tendency to generalize the effect of cannabis is being replaced with specific terpene percentages.

There are five chemotaxonomic types of cannabis. Hemp plants are fibrous *sativa* varieties and produces fewer resin flowers (about eighty less terpenes). Cannabis is typically sold as sativa, indica, or hybrid. However, the difference in effect comes from a combination of potency and pungency, or a combination of various cannabinoids, terpenes, terpenoids and flavinoids.

"Hemp" is a term used to classify fibrous cannabis varieties having a minute amount of THC (below 0.3%) and containing small amounts of CBD. Hemp-based products don't contain enough THC to stimulate the entourage effect and are typically dramatically less effective.

Strain or variety is only part of the equation when determining effect. Growing conditions, part of the plant, and harvest time affect the development of trichomes and resulting effect. The chemical makeup of the same strain of cannabis depends on several factors: quality of soil, age of plant, as well as extraction and processing techniques. The same variety usually has similar effects, but effects can vary depending on minor differences in genetics, growing season, harvesting time, and the extraction or infusion process.

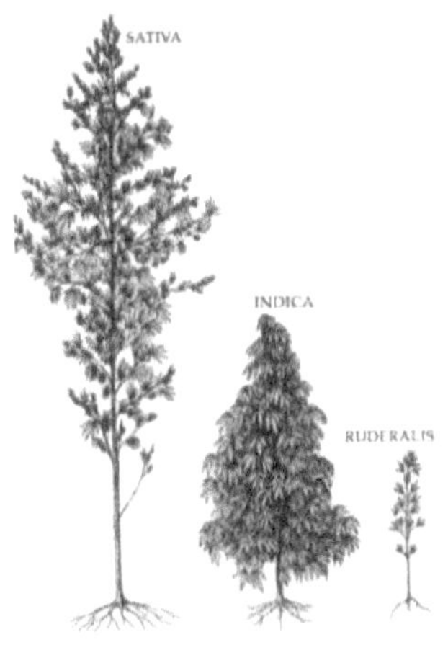

Entourage Effect & Whole Plant Full-Spectrum

The term "full-spectrum" describes dried or processed sun-grown whole plant medicine. Whole plant infused medicine uses the *entire* plant instead of isolated components. The most beneficially healing experience comes from consuming full-spectrum whole plant cannabis medicine.

The entourage effect is the mechanism behind whole plant medicine. Cannabinoids are enhanced by scent chemicals. Cannabis potency only accounts for part of the effect. Sedation, stimulation, euphoria, and other effects from different varieties of cannabis come from the fragrance or scent chemicals called terpenes.

There are over five hundred chemicals in whole cannabis plant medicine. Medical benefits come from complex interactions between chemicals. Cannabis contains more than cannabinoids. Terpenes and flavinoids are what provide flowers different scent and flavor. They play an important role in the survival of the plant by attracting pollinators and deterring predators. Terpenes interact with cannabinoids to enhance and balance the experience. There are over a hundred cannabinoids, twenty flavinoids, and two hundred terpenes in cannabis.

Certain chemicals work with each other as synergists while others counteract each other as antagonists. CBD and THC work synergistically to reduce pain and inflammation while antagonistically reducing anxiety and psychoactivity.

Cannabis dosing follows a biphasic dosing curve. Effects from cannabis follow a bell-curve, meaning a small dose of THC or CBD has similar effects to a large dose. There is greater autoinflammatory response and medicinal benefits peak at medium doses. The optimal dosing range is easier to determine, and users can reach peak medicinal effectiveness when using whole plant medicine.

When using cannabis, a balanced ratio of THC to CBD is suggested. Users are also encouraged to experiment with different amounts of THC and CBD to find their optimal ratio. THC and CBD interact with different cannabinoid receptors and areas of the body. When used together, patients find peak medicinal effectiveness by activating receptors, preventing cannabinoid breakdown, and stimulating both sides of the brain. THC and CBD together create harmony for systemic healing.

Raw or cold-processed cannabis is a powerful anti-inflammatory and mild pain killer with practically no side-effects for users. Medicinal users report cannabis products are more effective when containing an abundance of cannabinoids, terpenes, and flavonoids.

Children with seizures have reported the necessity linalool and THC in trace amounts when taking CBD medication. With five hundreddifferent chemicals in the cannabis plant, it is important to consume full-spectrum, whole plant medicine. Distilling or refining the plant into a single-molecule reduces peak medicinal qualities.

A standardized extract goes through the process of being distilled, refined, or isolated to guarantee the amount of a specific medicinal component. The intent of standardization is to provide consistency from batch-to-batch during manufacturing. Synthetic or pharmaceutical medicine is produced artificially in a lab based on a single chemical structure. Both standardized and synthetic medicine is less effective and harder to dose than whole plant medicine.

Scientists developed the practice of standardization and isolation to identify the components of medicinal plants that are pharmacologically active. Unfortunately, this method upsets the natural balance by attributing the effect of the whole plant to a single component. When concentrating one chemical at the expense of others, it unintentionally eliminates or neglects components that contribute to the entourage effect.

If medicating with refined or distilled products, it is important to take a reduced dosing curve into consideration. CBD or THC isolate and distillate is much harder to dose with. The biphasic curve is much smaller, effects are drastically reduced, and optimal dose is harder to determine. Rather than seeing an increase in medicinal value with an increase in consumption, the opposite occurs.

Increasing the dose of standardized medication does not improve the medicinal effect. Users can go from calm, relaxed, and happy to sedated, over-stimulated, or paranoid. Without a balance of cannabinoids, patients increase their risk for adverse side effects.

Distillates, extracts, and synthesized medicine are typically limited in the scope of treatment and often come with side-effects. Single molecules do not exhibit the entourage effect and have a smaller biphasic curve making it harder to determine the optimal dose.

Artisanal small-batch full spectrum products have become less widely available in California due to the erasure of small business under recreational legalization.

So how is it possible to determine which products are made with distillate? Some products will say "full plant spectrum" as a marketing gimmick. They can be distillated oils with a limited number of cannabis or botanical terpenes reintroduced—which is not the same quality as whole plant medicine. Cannabis derived terpenes are more expensive to produce, and some manufacturers use botanical terpenes to save cost and offer consistent products.

An easy way to tell by eye is to examine the color of your oil, tincture, capsule, or vape cartridge. Distilled oil stripped of many cannabinoids and terpenes are typically gold or clear in color. Products that are green or amber contain a full-spectrum profile.

Edibles will taste of cannabis if made with whole plant extracts. Chocolates and other edibles that have little or no cannabis flavor is made with standardized medicine.

Common Plant Cannabinoids

CBGA is the precursor to THCA, CBDA, and CBCA. Cannabis plants harvested early will have higher amounts of CBGA. Medicinal benefits include anti-inflammation.

CBG can be used for pain releif, inflammation, bacterial or fungal infection, bone growth, and inhibition of cell growth in certain cancer.

THCA is the precursor to delta-9 THC. It is found in raw cannabis. Medicinal benefits include anti-inflammatory, neuroprotective, anti-epileptic, and the inhibition of cell growth in tumors and certain cancer. THCA is far less psychoactive than THC and provides many similar benefits.

THCV is found in heated or aged cannabis. Medicinal benefits include suppressing the appetite, reducing seizures, reducing blood sugar levels, and prompting bone growth.

THC or delta-9 THC occurs when THCA is heated or aged. It is the psychoactive component of cannabis. Medicinal benefits include acute pain relief, appetite stimulation, reduction of vomiting and nausea, and suppression of muscle spasms.

CBN is the final stage of THC and is found in aged flower. Health effects of CBN include pain relief, reduction of muscle spasms, and anti-insomnia.

CBDA is the precursor to CBD and found in certain varieties of raw cannabis. Health benefits include anti-inflammatory and inhibition of tumor growth in certain cancer.

CBDV is found in heated or aged cannabis. Research has recently discovered it as a powerful anti-epileptic.

CBD is produced when CBDA is heated or aged. Medicinal benefits include pain relief, anti-inflammation, appetite stimulant, reduction of nausea and contractions in the small intestine, anxiety and depression relief, seizure reduction, suppression of muscle spasms, blood sugar regulation, anti-bacterial, promotion of bone growth, and inhibition of cell growth in tumors. People suffering from arthritis, MS, neuropathy pain, and neurodegeneration are encouraged to use CBD-rich medicine daily.

CBCA is the precursor to CBC and is found in raw cannabis. Medicinal uses include treatment for fungal infection and bacterial growth.

CBC is found in heated or aged cannabis. Medicinal benefits include pain relief, anti-inflammation, bone stimulant, and inhibition of cell growth in certain cancer.

Common Plant Terpenes

Camphene has the aroma of fir needles. It may help reduce cardiovascular disease.

Carene smells sweet and pungent and can be found in juniper berries. It is a central nervous system relaxant.

Caryophyllene has a strong citrus smell and activates certain CB receptors. It is found in bay leaves, black pepper, cloves, and cinnamon. Medical uses include inhibition of cancer tumor growth, anti-anxiety, anti-depressant, and addiction treatment. Caryophyllene binds to peripheral CB2 receptors in the skin and can be used as an anti-inflammatory topically.

Geraniol has a sweet smell like roses and shows promise in neuropathy treatment.

Humulene is found in hops and works to reduce nausea and as an anti-tumor, anti-bacterial, and anti-inflammatory. Humulene is known to suppress the appetite.

Limonene gives the aroma of lemons, limes, and oranges. Medicinal uses include increasing focus and attention, enhanced mood, gastrointestinal function improvement, ant-bacterial, and anti-fungal.

Linalool is found in lavender and has floral notes. Medicinal uses include sleep aid, anxiety and depression relief, and increased immune function.

Myrcene has a musky, earthy, herbal aroma found in mango, lemongrass, and thyme. It is a potent pain killer, anti-inflammatory, and anti-biotic. Myrcene is known to enhance the psychoactive effects of cannabinoids.

Terpineol is found in lilacs and has calming and relaxing effects. Terpineol is an acne inhibitor and works to boost anti-oxidants.

Terpinolene has a combination of pine and floral notes. Health benefits include drowsiness, allowing it to function as a aid sleep.

Pinene smells like pine needles and is found in rosemary, basil, and parsley. Health benefits include anti-inflammation and bronchodilation. Pinene promotes alertness and memory retention.

First Time Use

During first time use, there can be little to no effect. Even after trying a few times, some patients may not be aware of feeling a difference, but those around them will notice a more relaxed and happy state of being. It's difficult to determine what to expect.

Medicine typically needs to be taken regularly for some patients to be able to feel the effects. ECS receptors may need time to develop or reset if dysfunctional. CBD can take up to three weeks of regular use before reaching peak effectiveness.

For the first few times, it is best to limit THC between 1 to 5mg. CBD is non-psychoactive for most users and can be taken up to 10mg. Test for any sedating, stimulating, or mind-altering effects with new cannabis products in a comfortable space with enough time to experience effects uninterrupted.

There is no standard dose, delivery method, length of use, or variety of cannabis to find the optimal dose for homeostasis. It is up to each user to use intuition and experimentation to find their optimal dose. Remember moderation helps maintain the optimal dosage by preventing tolerance from building.

Choosing Medicine

With many cannabis products to choose from, it takes education and experimentation to find what's best. An understanding of terpenes, cannabinoids, and methods for consumption helps patients know what to expect and allows you to choose the most effective product.

First consider what effect you're looking to obtain before choosing a cannabis product. A significant consideration is the active ingredient. This is easiest to find on the label as THC or CBD in milligrams or as a percentage. Ratios can be confusing, and it is best to determine how many milligrams of each active ingredient is in each individual serving.

To decide which strain to smoke or vaporize, smell through different varieties of dried cannabis flowers. Each strain will invite or detour your nose.

When purchasing any commercial product for consumption, there are certain quality standards to ensure safety. Look for a batch number, manufacture or expiration date, contact information, ingredients, potency in milligram, and terpene profile.

Pets and children should receive medicine that is high in CBD and low in THC. Anyone looking to avoid psychoactivity should choose products low in THC. CBD can be used to counteract unintended anxiety associated with THC use.

Dosing

All medicine is highly individualized. Whole plant medicine and pharmaceuticals have a range of dosages and are not one size fits all. Patients with the same condition can respond differently to medicine—even when using the same method, strain, and dosage. Each person has a unique biochemistry, endocannabinoid system, and DNA that respond differently to cannabis.

Safely and successfully experiment with the many options available by using observation to gauge physical and mental reactions. Keeping a journal of plant use helps find the optimal method and dose. Most patients find it doesn't take much to feel at ease. During intense recovery, some patients might take higher doses at first to regain balance. Once health and harmony are established, micro and moderate dosing can be used as prevention and maintenance.

Starting low and going slow when dosing is the best suggested method to find the optimal amount of medicine. Start with low doses of THC and CBD and only increase the dose after a few days or weeks of use. This method prevents intense psychoactivity, decreases side-effects, and prevents building tolerance. Users clearly establish a dose that helps relieve stress and pain without ever going overboard. Large or macro-doses are better suited for experienced users with chronic or terminal illnesses.

It can be beneficial to cut back or abstain periodically to reset receptors if using cannabis regularly as part of the recovery process. Taking a few days per week or one week off per month helps receptors from receding. Micro and standard doses can be maintained as part of a moderate lifestyle. If a cannabis user maintains a large intake of medicine for stress or pain relief, then our neuroreceptors adapt and tolerance builds. Periodic abstinence or micro-dosing allows users to and avoid building a tolerance.

Micro-dosing can be effective for creativity, energy, focus, insomnia, headaches, euphoria, anxiety, mild pain, and basic metabolic or blood sugar disorders. A micro-dose is generally one to two milligrams but can be up to ten milligrams for experienced users.

Standard or moderate doses aid with inflammation, depression, moderate pain, menstrual cramps, autoimmune disease, gastrointestinal disorders, neurodegenerative disease, heart disease, seizures, migraines, and autism. A standard dose is generally between five to twenty-five milligrams.

Macro-dosing is used to treat epilepsy, severe addiction, cancer, liver disease, severe pain, post-traumatic stress, organ failure, and life-threatening conditions. A macro-dose is typically anything over fifty milligrams.

Methods of Consumption

Our body absorbs medicine differently depending on the variety, method, dose, metabolism, mood, and level of pain. Diet plays an important role. Research has shown a large variability in bioavailability of cannabinoids when smoking cannabis, while controlling the length of inhalation, hold time, exhalation time, and time between puffs. Beta-caryophyllene, omegas, and other chemicals that can be found in our diet interact with the ECS.

Certain foods increase the bioavailability of THC and cannabinoids. Plant medicine is commonly infused into chocolate. Raw cacao provides anandamide, antioxidants, and acts as support for enhanced absorption with exceptional amounts of magnesium, zinc, Vitimin C, omega-6, fiber, and chromium.

Edibles are processed through the liver and convert into a more psychoactive and sedative Delta-11 THC. Edibles can hit stronger when taken on an empty stomach. Raw cannabis that is non-psychoactive can decarboxylate if your stomach is full of food. Micro-dosing gives most users a functional high. Increasing the dose leads to increased psychoactivity, dry mouth, and possible negative side effects. Terpenes are mostly lost during cooking or manufactured using distillates. Edibles are mostly labeled as *Sativa* or *Indica* as a marketing gimmick.

Digestion slows down when consuming cannabis, creating an onset time of thirty minutes to two hours. Effects can last up to eight hours. Bioavailability of medicine varies between 8-15%

Tinctures made from ethanol have the highest absorption rate and avoid liver digestion. Oil-based tinctures are useful for users looking to avoid alcohol but can be mostly processed as an edible. Oil tinctures high in omegas can be partially absorbed under the tongue if left for three to ten minutes. Ethanol can be diluted in juice or water to avoid burning the mucous membrane. Cannabis tinctures are especially helpful for people suffering from asthma. Cannabinoids are a potent bronchodilator and help smooth muscle relax. Just a few drops under the tongue help open the airway.

Onset for effects from sublingual dosing takes fifteen minutes to an hour. Effects typically last between four and six hours with a bioavailability of 6-20%

Topicals are applied directly to the skin for local relief. Effects are immediate and last from four to six hours. Topical do not enter the bloodstream and are non-psychoactive by nature. Washing your hands after application and avoiding cuts will prevent cannabinoids from passing through skin. Topicals interact with CB and TRP receptors in the skin to regulate epidermal homeostasis. Users have reported THC and THCA being effective for pain relief and inflammation. CBD has been found useful for skin disorders and burns.

Transdermal patches only work if the molecules are small enough to enter the bloodstream. Chemical permeation enhancers are added in pharmaceutical-grade patches and are not commercially available.

Onset for effects from transdermal dosing takes fifteen minutes. Effects can last up to twelve hours with an unknown bioavailability.

Vaporization is the safer alternative to smoking cannabis and eliminates many health risks associated with combustion. The benefits of inhaling plant medicine include immediate relief, increased effectiveness, and controlled dosing.

Suppositories are a good option for patients who have trouble keeping food down and are looking to avoid smoking or vaporization. People suffering endometritis, prostate or rectal cancer, menstrual cramps, hemorrhoids, and gastrointestinal disorders find localized and systemic relief when used rectally or vaginally. Insert suppositories far enough to keep it in, but not *too* far, as that can lead to liver digestion and increased effects. Bioavailability for suppositories is somewhat unknown as few studies have been done and pharmaceutical suppositories have enhancers for molecule absorption.

Crafting Cannabis

Quality cannabis flower results in quality medicine when manufactured under certain conditions. Certain solvents and methods maintain the complex full-spectrum found in raw cannabis flower.

Homogenization is the process of continual mixing to evenly distribute medicine. It takes a bit of chemistry and creativity to be able to homogenize cannabis into a fat source.

Cannabis is non-psychoactive until heated. Cannabinoids undergo chemical changes over time when exposed to light and heat. Decarboxylation is the process of adding heat to cannabis to activate different components. Chemical composition and effect vary depending on the length of time and heat added to the plant. To activate the most amount of cannabinoids, heat cannabis flower in a covered glass baking dish for thirty minutes at 250°F and leave to cool before processing.

By heating cannabis at a lower temperature, it takes more time but preserves more terpenes and cannabinoids.

Recipes

Cannabis can be crafted or manufactured using different methods. Low heat allows for a slower infusion process. High heat speeds up the process but requires more care and concentration. Cold processed cannabis provides an array of health benefits without the psychoactivity or high.

<u>Oil</u>

Ingredients:

- 2-5 cups cold-pressed olive, avocado, grapeseed, sunflower, sesame, macadamia, or safflower oil
- 7-14 grams (per cup) ground cannabis

Equipment:

- Glass jar
- Cheesecloth

Instructions:

- Decarboxylate cannabis if desired.
- Fill jar with cannabis and cover with oil.
- Store out of sunlight in a cool place for 4-6 weeks. Shake every 3 days.
- Strain. Store in dark glass bottle.

Tincture

Ingredients:

- 2-5 cups grain alcohol (151 or 190 proof) or vegetable glycerin
- 7-28 grams per cup ground cannabis
- Cheesecloth

Equipment:

- Glass jar
- Caution as alcohol is highly flammable.

Instructions:

- Decarboxylate cannabis if desired.
- Fill glass jar with cannabis. Cover with alcohol or glycerin.
- Store out of sunlight in a cool 4-6 weeks. Shake every 3 days.
- Strain through cheesecloth into dark glass bottle.

Full Extract Cannabis Oil (Rick Simpson Oil)

Instructions: Hazardous—Use caution!

- Slowly heat 1-5 cups of ethanol cannabis tincture on an induction or hot plate. Do not use an open flame. Warm or low simmer for 30-45 minutes per cup of alcohol, constantly stirring until it becomes a sticky syrup. Cool for one minute and quickly pour into a dark glass bottle. Cook in a well-ventilated area.

Cautions

Cannabis is non-toxic, and no lethal dose has ever occurred. No brain or organ damage has been reported in studies. Long-term exposure to cannabis does not cause persistent cognitive deficits nor schizophrenia in adults. CB receptors do not control breathing and heart rate as opioids do.

THC causes an increased heart rate of 20-50bpm. Patients with heart conditions and on prescription medicine should discuss cannabis use with their doctor. An overdose cannot kill you but can cause adverse reaction and possibly a feeling of panic. When over-stimulated, the ECS can trigger or worsen the symptom that would otherwise be relieved when using the optimal dose. Unnecessary stress can be avoided through micro-dosing.

THCA and CBD are commonly said to be non-psychoactive. Most users report no change in behavior. However, a minority of users experience CBD similar to caffeine. Symptoms reported include hyperactivity, diarrhea, and restlessness. Macro doses produce sedating effects. Test new cannabis products in small amounts for sensitivity. All side effects from cannabis can be resolved with changes in delivery method, ratio, variety, or dosing.

As cannabis absorbs fungicides, herbicides, and insecticides, it should be tested for purity to avoid cancer, skin irritation, neurologic disorders, reproductive problems, and other disorders. Conscious practices and lab testing ensure the final product is free of pesticides, toxins, heavy metals, containments, pests, mold and mildew. Contaminated medicine may be toxic, especially to patients with a compromised immune system.

Using products that have high levels of toxins or residual solvents can cause hyperemesis or an allergic and possibly severe reaction to contaminated medicine. Symptoms include headache and vomiting. Solvents used to manufacture cannabis products and concentrates can be made using carcinogenic neurotoxins such as butane, propane, or hexane.

Concentrating contaminated plant matter increases the risk of side effects. Concentrates and vape cartridges can contain added toxic substances, additives or thinners with unknown long-term effects. Solvents and toxic additives can lead to headaches, nervous system depression, nausea, dizziness, and other possible adverse side effects when consumed. Pure cannabis oil is the safest product to vaporize. Any side effect can be eliminated by eliminating product use.

Tolerance can build if using cannabis regularly. Periodic abstinence from use helps maintain gratitude, balance, and optimal dosage by preventing receptors from receding inside cell walls from over-stimulation.

Patients who suffer if discontinuing cannabis use generally farm plants for personal use in order to avoid the cost of having to continually increase dosage.

Driving

New users driving under the influence of THC have a lack of tracking ability, attentiveness, judgment, peripheral vision, and coordination. Driving should be avoided for up to eight hours. Many users report a heightened sense of focus while using cannabis and joke about being attentive for police. Under mild to moderate doses of THC, most drivers still over-compensate, can be easily distracted, or react slower than normal.

Alcohol

It is not advised to mix cannabis and alcohol. Edibles are processed through the liver and should be avoided with alcohol. Coordination and extreme disorientation are possible as alcohol increases the absorption of THC.

Pregnancy & Nursing

Cannabis use in pregnant women is socially frowned upon. Instead of using cannabis medicine during labor, many women receive an epidural without realizing it's a synthetic derivative of cocaine with potential negative side effects.

There has been no evidence of difference in growth of the fetus or development of the newborn for cannabis-using mothers. In fact, the ECS is involved in regulating many of the chemical messengers in fertility and breastfeeding. For women with naturally low levels of anandamide, CBD can help increase the possibility of pregnancy. This does not mean pregnant and nursing mothers should use cannabis heavily.

Exercise, massage, stretching, and a balanced diet before, during, and after pregnancy should be the priority. Nausea and excess stress from tension in mothers can cause harm on the fetus. Excess weight loss from morning sickness can lead to malnutrition.

Every patient needs to outweigh the benefits with possible risks and avoid any possible harm by using cannabis sparingly and in small amounts to decrease nausea and pain. Breast milk contains endocannabinoids and will carry phytocannabinoids as well. However, cannabis can be used to replace missing cannabinoids in the breastmilk of postpartum mothers.

Children and Minors

For children with mental or physical illness, regaining a balanced and functioning ECS is critical for development. The benefits of using cannabinoid medicine under supervision and in moderation far outweighs the risks in some cases. Children with autism, ADHD, cancer, diabetes, seizures, and Tourette syndrome have all found relief without the side effects associated with pharmaceuticals. Mild and moderate cannabis use hasn't been reported to show any negative long-term effects. Heavy use can lead to psychological dependency.

For healthy children and minors in a stable nurturing environment, it is important that they avoid or limit the use of any drug during brain development.

Pharmaceuticals

If taking any prescription drug, you should investigate if there are possible interactions with cannabis and speak with your doctor prior to using medicinal herbs. Certain drugs may require a smaller dose when taking plant supplements. CBD can increase or decrease the breakdown of other medication.

RX interactions are notes in the following drugs: AEDs, steroids, Ca channel blockers, antihistamines, prokinetics, HIV antiviral, immune modulators, benzodiazepines, anti-arrythmics, antibiotics, antipsychotics, antidepressants, anti-elliptics, beta blockers, NSAIDs, PPIs

Drug Testing

Cannabinoids are excreted through feces and urine in approximately three to five days. Remnants can also be stored in the fatty tissue for regular users and take around three weeks to eliminate all traces of phytocannabinoids.

Smoking

Cannabinoids bind to the carcinogenic protein caused by smoke, making potential cancer risks unknown.

Vaporization of cannabis flower is the safest suggested method to medicate. It allows users to avoid carcinogenic chemicals caused by combustion.

Smudging is the burning of herbs and plants as a method of purification to balance the physical body and atmosphere. Ceremonies with smoke are used to carry thoughts and prayers into the spirit world. When we inhale smoke, we ourselves are thought to be cleansed as we embark on a journey to the spirit world and come back reborn.

The science behind hot-boxing, secondhand smoke, and essential oil diffusers explains this phenomenon. When releasing smoke into the air, we inhale minimal amounts of the particulates. Certain smells cause us to feel relaxed, energized, hungry, or clear our sinuses. When releasing herbs with scent or psychoactive components, we inhale trace amounts and experience an effect.

While there is no conclusive evidence that smoking cannabis is detrimental, weigh the risks and benefits and try vaporization as an alternative.

Nicotine receptors share the same receptors as THC, and smoking tobacco limits the effect of cannabis. Try a balanced ratio of CBD and THC, instead of the combination of tobacco and cannabis flower, if the goal is to moderate psychoactive effects.

Experimental Field Notes

The following pages can be used to help track cannabis use. Keeping a journal can be helpful for cannabis users to track the effects of different products, strains, or home-made remedies.

Experimental Field Notes

Date: _____________ Time: _______________

Dose: __________ Method: _____________

Strain/Product: _________________________

Last Meal: ☐ Light ☐ Moderate ☐ Heavy
When: ☐ 1 hr ☐ 2 hrs ☐ 3+ hrs

Desired effect: ☐ Pain Relief ☐ Euphoria
☐ Relaxation ☐ Reduce cravings ☐ Appetite
☐ Focus ☐ Energy ☐ Creativity ☐ Sleep
☐ _________________________________

Pain level: _______   Stress level: ______

0 1 2 3 4 5 6 7 8 9 10

Intensity Graph:

Strong

Optimal

Weak

15m   30m   1hr   2hrs   3hrs   4hrs   5hrs

Experimental Field Notes

Phytocannabinoids: ☐ THCA ☐ THC ☐ THCV
☐ CBD ☐ CBG ☐ CBC ☐ CBN ☐ CBDA
☐ Delta-8 THC ☐ Beta-caryophyllene
☐ ______________________________

Terpenes: ☐ Humulene ☐ Limonene ☐ Pinene
☐ Linalool ☐ Myrcene ☐ Terpinolene
☐ Geraneol ☐ Nerolidol ☐ Ocimene ☐ Terpineol
☐ ______________________________

Diet: ☐ Beta-caryophyllene ☐ Anti-inflammatories
☐ Pro-biotics ☐ Omegas ☐ Adaptogens
☐ Antioxidants
☐ ______________________________

Daily Activity: ☐ Light ☐ Moderate ☐ Intense

Experience: ______________________________

____

____

Side Effects: ☐ Dry mouth ☐ Over-stimulated
☐ Drowsy ☐ Lethargic ☐ Paranoia
☐ ______________________________

Desired Effect: ☐ Yes ☐ No ☐ ______________

Rating: ☆ ☆ ☆ ☆ ☆

Experimental Field Notes

Date: _____________   Time: _______________

Dose: ___________   Method: ____________

Strain/Product: _______________________

Last Meal: ☐ Light ☐ Moderate ☐ Heavy
When: ☐ 1 hr ☐ 2 hrs ☐ 3+ hrs

Desired effect: ☐ Pain Relief ☐ Euphoria
☐ Relaxation ☐ Reduce cravings ☐ Appetite
☐ Focus ☐ Energy ☐ Creativity ☐ Sleep
☐ _______________________________

Pain level: _______   Stress level: ______

0 1 2 3 4 5 6 7 8 9 10

Intensity Graph:

Strong

Optimal

Weak

15m   30m   1hr   2hrs   3hrs   4hrs   5hrs

Experimental Field Notes

Phytocannabinoids: ☐ THCA ☐ THC ☐ THCV
☐ CBD ☐ CBG ☐ CBC ☐ CBN ☐ CBDA
☐ Delta-8 THC ☐ Beta-caryophyllene
☐ ___________________________

Terpenes: ☐ Humulene ☐ Limonene ☐ Pinene
☐ Linalool ☐ Myrcene ☐ Terpinolene
☐ Geraneol ☐ Nerolidol ☐ Ocimene ☐ Terpineol
☐ ___________________________

Diet: ☐ Beta-caryophyllene ☐ Anti-inflammatories
☐ Pro-biotics ☐ Omegas ☐ Adaptogens
☐ Antioxidants
☐ ___________________________

Daily Activity: ☐ Light ☐ Moderate ☐ Intense

Experience:___________________________

____

____

Side Effects: ☐ Dry mouth ☐ Over-stimulated
☐ Drowsy ☐ Lethargic ☐ Paranoia
☐ ___________________________

Desired Effect: ☐ Yes ☐ No ☐ ___________

Rating: ☆ ☆ ☆ ☆ ☆

Part III: Using Cannabis

Experimental Field Notes

Date: _______________   Time: _________________

Dose: _____________   Method: _____________

Strain/Product: _______________________________

Last Meal: ☐ Light ☐ Moderate ☐ Heavy
When: ☐ 1 hr ☐ 2 hrs ☐ 3+ hrs

Desired effect: ☐ Pain Relief ☐ Euphoria
☐ Relaxation ☐ Reduce cravings ☐ Appetite
☐ Focus ☐ Energy ☐ Creativity ☐ Sleep
☐ _______________________________

Pain level: _______   Stress level: ______

0   1   2   3   4   5   6   7   8   9   10

Intensity Graph:

Strong

Optimal

Weak

15m   30m   1hr   2hrs   3hrs   4hrs   5hrs

Experimental Field Notes

Phytocannabinoids: ☐ THCA ☐ THC ☐ THCV
☐ CBD ☐ CBG ☐ CBC ☐ CBN ☐ CBDA
☐ Delta-8 THC ☐ Beta-caryophyllene
☐ _________________________________

Terpenes: ☐ Humulene ☐ Limonene ☐ Pinene
☐ Linalool ☐ Myrcene ☐ Terpinolene
☐ Geraneol ☐ Nerolidol ☐ Ocimene ☐ Terpineol
☐ _________________________________

Diet: ☐ Beta-caryophyllene ☐ Anti-inflammatories
☐ Pro-biotics ☐ Omegas ☐ Adaptogens
☐ Antioxidants
☐ _________________________________

Daily Activity: ☐ Light ☐ Moderate ☐ Intense

Experience:_________________________________

____

____

Side Effects: ☐ Dry mouth ☐ Over-stimulated
☐ Drowsy ☐ Lethargic ☐ Paranoia
☐ _________________________________

Desired Effect: ☐ Yes ☐ No ☐ _________________

Rating: ☆☆☆☆☆

Experimental Field Notes

Date: _____________ Time: _______________

Dose: _____________ Method: _____________

Strain/Product: _________________________

Last Meal: ☐ Light ☐ Moderate ☐ Heavy
When: ☐ 1 hr ☐ 2 hrs ☐ 3+ hrs

Desired effect: ☐ Pain Relief ☐ Euphoria
☐ Relaxation ☐ Reduce cravings ☐ Appetite
☐ Focus ☐ Energy ☐ Creativity ☐ Sleep
☐ _____________________________

Pain level: _______   Stress level: ______

Intensity Graph:

Strong

Optimal

Weak

          15m   30m   1hr   2hrs   3hrs   4hrs   5hrs

Experimental Field Notes

Phytocannabinoids: ☐ THCA ☐ THC ☐ THCV
☐ CBD ☐ CBG ☐ CBC ☐ CBN ☐ CBDA
☐ Delta-8 THC ☐ Beta-caryophyllene
☐ ______________________________

Terpenes: ☐ Humulene ☐ Limonene ☐ Pinene
☐ Linalool ☐ Myrcene ☐ Terpinolene
☐ Geraneol ☐ Nerolidol ☐ Ocimene ☐ Terpineol
☐ ______________________________

Diet: ☐ Beta-caryophyllene ☐ Anti-inflammatories
☐ Pro-biotics ☐ Omegas ☐ Adaptogens
☐ Antioxidants
☐ ______________________________

Daily Activity: ☐ Light ☐ Moderate ☐Intense

Experience:______________________________

____

____

Side Effects: ☐ Dry mouth ☐ Over-stimulated
☐ Drowsy ☐ Lethargic ☐ Paranoia
☐ ______________________________

Desired Effect: ☐ Yes ☐ No ☐ ___________

Rating: ☆☆☆☆☆

Recommended Resources

For more information on dosing and specific medical conditions aided by cannabis:
Cannabis Health Index by Uwe Blesching

For more information on cannabis laws and obtaining a medical recommendation:
www.SafeAccessNow.org

For more information on scientific research:
National Library of Medicine Online

For more information on growing cannabis:
Marijuana Growers Handbook by Ed Rosenthal

For more information on addiction:
Refuge Recovery by Noah Levine

For more information on positive thinking:
Power Choices by Dr. Brenda Wade
The Places That Scare You by Pema Chödrön

Epilogue

Cannabis was stigmatized to enable suppression and imprisonment of people of color. The United States patented cannabis as an antioxidant and neuroprotectant while simultaneously imprisoning people for its use. As the *Refer Madness* era comes to an end, there are still many people unaware of the medical benefits of cannabis. Is there a line between medicinal, therapeutic, or recreational use?

Getting high refers to entering a blissful state of physical and mental relaxation. Anyone experiencing pain or emotional suffering has times they feel low. Cannabis is used therapeutically when enabling users to experience happiness.

The more serious the illness, the more commitment it takes to restore balance. Lifestyle changes and multiple therapies help healing occur.

Tools like plant diet, massage, music, meditation, and enjoyable exercise can be used to enhance our endocannabinoid system, increase effectiveness of plant medicine, and restore balance. Harmony is built on a foundation of positive thinking and healthy habits.

For people trapped by victimizing or self-harming behavior, chasing the high and release of chemicals associated with bliss becomes burdensome. There is a line between use and abuse. We all must work to enjoy life in many ways and use chemical substances in moderation.

Questions or Comments?

Email: CannabisManual@gmail.com